Accelerated learning in the Literacy Hour

Year 6

Sue Garnett

CONTENTS

Page	Section	Kinaesthetic	Auditory	Visual
3	INTRODUCTION			
8	Modern retelling	Make a comic strip	Creating gossip about a saint	Write a news report
13	Playscripts	Make a concertina playscript	Act it out	Publish a book
18	Biographies	Make a wall display	Hot seating	Make a wanted poster
23	News reports	Prepare a radio report	Make an interview	Write a report
28	Science fiction genre	Making and using cutouts	Make a live report	Write a diary
33	Flashbacks	Retelling a flashback	Using music	Using a picture
38	Points of view	Produce a poster	Make a telephone call	Write a letter
43	Official language	Act it out	Plan and hold a telephone conversation	Write a letter
48	Writing blurb	Create blurb for a film	Be a film critic	Write some book blurb
53	Extended stories	Write a story then mime it	Write a story for the radio	Make a real book
58	Explanations	Make a labelled display on conductors	Demonstrate static electricity	Make an arrow chart about magnets
63	Non-chronological reports	Make a wall display	Hold a debate	Produce an OHT

Published by Hopscotch Educational Publishing Ltd,
Unit 2, The Old Brushworks, 56 Pickwick Road, Corsham, Wiltshire, SN13 9BX (Tel: 01249 701701)

© 2002 Hopscotch Educational Publishing

Written by Susan Garnett
Series design by Blade Communications
Illustrated by Catherine Ward
Cover illustration by Debbie Clark
Printed by Clintplan, Southam

ISBN 1-904307-15-9

Susan Garnett hereby asserts her moral right to be identified as the author of this work in accordance with the Copyright, Designs and Patents Act, 1988.

All rights reserved. This book is sold subject to the condition that it shall not, by way of trade or otherwise, be lent, hired out or otherwise circulated without the publisher's prior consent in any form of binding or cover other than that in which it is published and without a similar condition, including this condition, being imposed upon the subsequent purchaser.

No part of this publication may be reproduced, stored in a retrieval system, or transmitted, in any form or by any means, electronic, mechanical, photocopying, recording or otherwise, without the prior permission of the publisher, except where photocopying for educational purposes within the school or other educational establishment that has purchased this book is expressly permitted in the text.

INTRODUCTION

ACCELERATED LEARNING IN THE LITERACY HOUR

This series of books and the activity ideas are a direct result of the research into brain-based learning and multiple intelligences, how the brain works and how children learn. Alistair Smith sets out the results of this research in his books *Accelerated Learning in the Classroom* and *Accelerated Learning in Practice* (published by Network Educational Press Ltd). Information from his research and these books is given below.

Visual, Auditory and Kinaesthetic Learning (VAK)

People learn using their senses: their sense of hearing, sight and touch.

- 29% of us prefer to learn by seeing.
- 34% of us prefer to learn by hearing and using sound.
- 37% of us prefer to learn by doing.

It is important to know which is our preference, but it is just as important to learn to use the other senses too.

If we are to maximise children's learning, we should be aware of the children's strengths and not only provide them with activities that they prefer, but also give them access to all three types of learning so that they will learn new skills.

We remember:
- 20% of what we see
- 30% of what we hear
- 40% of what we say
- 50% of what we do
- 90% of what we see, hear, say and do.

Therefore, it is vital that you deliver lessons in such a way that there is variety, i.e. by using visual, auditory and kinaesthetic activities. You should provide input that covers all three types of learning. This may be done during the course of a lesson or over a series of lessons.

It is important that you provide a balanced curriculum covering the three types of learning just as you would provide a balanced diet.

Multiple Intelligences (MI)

Howard Gardner identified the Seven Plus One Intelligences (this has now become the Nine Intelligences). He said that people have different types of intelligences and that they are better at some than others. All the Nine Intelligences are important. All children are intelligent in some way.

The Nine Intelligences are:
- logical (Number/order smart)
- linguistic (Word smart)
- visual/spatial (Picture smart)
- interpersonal (People smart)
- intrapersonal (Myself smart)
- physical (Body smart)
- naturalistic (Naturalistic smart)
- musical (Music smart)
- spiritual.

Children benefit from a balance of activities which can enhance their preferred learning style. But it is also important to introduce them to other types of learning to strengthen and develop those with which they are not as confident. Providing a range and balance of activities will maximise their learning.

A balanced approach to learning

Visual, auditory and kinaesthetic learning fit in really well with the Nine Intelligences.

Example

Lesson objective – To prepare a short section of a story as a script in the form of a concertina book.
The children would be learning kinaesthetically.
The children would also be using several of the Nine Intelligences, i.e. physical, linguistic, visual/spatial and intrapersonal.

What is this book?

This book is a teacher resource. It provides a series of ideas to use in the classroom that will develop and maximise children's learning.

It provides visual, auditory and kinaesthetic activities to achieve the text level objectives of the National Literacy Strategy.

It also includes references to the Nine Intelligences.

This book will help towards enabling ALL children to be successful. It helps you to reach all of the children more of the time.

How does this book work?

Each lesson plan contains a literacy objective (text level), a whole class starter activity, ideas for group work (visual, auditory and kinaesthetic activities) and a plenary session. Each lesson also contains three sheets:

Sheet 1
This is a model that you share with the children.

Sheet 2
This sheet gives information on the three activities (visual, auditory and kinaesthetic) that you can use with the children to achieve the objective. You could split the children into groups according to their preferred learning style, or cover all the activities over a period of time. Children with special educational needs could cover the style they are most likely to be successful with.

Sheet 3
This is the children's worksheet. They may use it to make notes or plan their work.

If there are adult helpers in the class, they can work with a group of children on one of the objectives.

Recognising children's preferred learning styles

Below are lists of activities that the different types of learner enjoy doing. Over a period of time, teachers should try to ensure that children receive a balance from each list.

VISUAL LEARNERS

They learn best through seeing.

How can you recognise a visual learner?
They speak with their hands. They like to point things out. They speak rapidly.

What do they enjoy?
- Writing
- Drawing
- Computers
- OHPs
- Television
- Posters
- News reports
- Books
- Diaries
- Letters
- Key words
- Wall displays
- Films/videos
- Interactive whiteboards
- Interactive displays
- Arrow charts
- Flow charts
- Graphs
- Diagrams
- Pictures
- Mind maps

INTRODUCTION

AUDITORY LEARNERS

They learn best through sound.

How can you recognise an auditory learner?
They like to hum, sing or whistle while doing activities. They like to give and receive instructions verbally.

What do they enjoy?
- Audio tapes/CDs
- Radio programmes
- Circle time
- Hot seating
- Lectures
- Show and tell
- Debates/discussion
- School council
- Points of view
- Music and sound effects
- Interviews/interviewing
- Reporting
- Dance
- Drama

KINAESTHETIC LEARNERS

They learn best through movement.

How can you recognise a kinaesthetic learner?
They like to move about the classroom and touch things. They get restless sitting down. They like physical activities. They like to demonstrate or model. They fidget.

What do they enjoy?
- Role play and dressing up
- Show and tell
- Making things
- Modelling and collage
- Murals
- Puppet and mask making
- Flap books and concertina books
- Outdoor lessons
- Field trips
- Outdoor pursuits
- PE
- Dance
- Gym
- Music and Movement
- Brain gym
- Performances

How to find out what type of learner a child is

On page 6 there is a questionnaire. The children can either be given this to complete themselves or be helped by an adult to complete it.

The key to the questionnaire is given on page 7. For example, if the answer given to the first question by a child is 'Yes' then that indicates 'kinaesthetic'.

The results may show that the child has a dominant learning style or they may show that he or she has several learning styles.

The idea is to provide you, the teacher, with valuable information about the children so that you are better able to help them with their learning.

INTRODUCTION

What kind of learner am I?

Name _____   Class _____

1. I like making things.	Yes	No
2. I like watching films.	Yes	No
3. I like listening to music.	Yes	No
4. I like listening to story tapes.	Yes	No
5. I like designing posters.	Yes	No
6. I like acting.	Yes	No
7. I like sport and playing out.	Yes	No
8. I like drawing.	Yes	No
9. I like lessons outdoors.	Yes	No
10. I like school trips.	Yes	No
11. I like dancing.	Yes	No
12. I like writing.	Yes	No
13. I like talking.	Yes	No
14. I like show and tell.	Yes	No
15. I like speaking in front of others.	Yes	No
16. I like debating and discussing.	Yes	No
17. I like drawing diagrams.	Yes	No
18. I like looking at the blackboard.	Yes	No
19. I like using whiteboards.	Yes	No
20. I like to talk while I work.	Yes	No
21. I like moving about.	Yes	No
22. I like reading.	Yes	No

INTRODUCTION

What kind of learner am I?
(Answer key)

1. K
2. V
3. A
4. A
5. V
6. K
7. K
8. V
9. K
10. K
11. K
12. V
13. A
14. A
15. A
16. A
17. V
18. V
19. V
20. A
21. K
22. V

Count how many of each type they have.

> **Example**
> Jack Barnes   Class 6
>
> Visual = 0
> Auditory = 3
> Kinaesthetic = 6
>
> Dominant learning style = kinaesthetic

If a child circles all the yes answers, then they have no preferred learning style.

If they circle yes to 1, 6, 7, 9, 10, 11, 21 then they are a kinaesthetic learner.

If they circle yes to 2, 5, 8, 12, 17, 18, 19, 22 then they are a visual learner.

If they circle yes to 3, 4, 13, 14, 15, 16, 20 then they are an auditory learner.

Most children have a dominant learning style. If you give them the appropriate type of learning activity, then they will learn. For example, give a kinaesthetic learner things to make and things to do.

It is also important to give children a variety of activities not just those from their own preferred learning style in order that they develop new skills.

Children can be told what kind of learner they are. If they understand how they learn best, they can help themselves.

TEACHER'S NOTES

Modern retelling

Literacy objective
- To manipulate narrative perspective by producing a modern retelling.

What you need
- Photocopies of pages 10 and 12
- A3 paper
- Stories about famous saints
- A tape recorder
- Religious books (for example, the Bible, the Koran, the Guru Granth Sahib)
- Coloured pens or pencils

Whole class starter

- Give each child a copy of the 'George and the wolf' sheet on page 10 or display it on an OHP or interactive whiteboard.

- Tell the children that they are going to work on a modern retelling of a story. What do they think is meant by a modern retelling? Encourage them to share their ideas but do not come to any agreement yet. Explain that they may have some more ideas about settings after sharing a text together.

- Together, read the story 'George and the wolf'.

- Ask the children the following questions.
   - What is the story about?
   - This is a modern retelling of a story. The original story was about a famous saint who killed a dragon. What is the famous story? (St George and the dragon)
   - How is the plot of the story the same?
   - How has it been altered to make it modern?
   - What other old stories do you know? (For example, ones about saints, stories from the Bible, the Koran, and other religious books)

- Look at one or two examples from the religious texts. How could these stories be retold to make them modern? What differences would there be (modern names, lifestyles such as using shops, cars and technology)?

- Ask the children how they think the language is different in a modern retelling.

8   ACCELERATED LEARNING – YEAR 6

Teacher's Notes

Independent/group work

From the activities on page 11, either:

- select the most appropriate activity for each child/group according to whether they are kinaesthetic, auditory or visual learners and organise three separate working groups

or

- begin with the kinaesthetic activity for the whole class, then progress to the auditory and finally the visual activity over several lessons.

Tell the children that they are now going to do more work about modern retellings.

The kinaesthetic learners will need:
sheets of A3 paper, copies of the 'My modern retelling' sheet on page 12, copies of the story of David and Goliath from the bible and coloured pens or pencils.

The auditory learners will need:
stories about famous saints, copies of the 'My modern retelling' sheet on page 12 and a tape recorder.

The visual learners will need:
some religious books (for example, the Bible, the Koran, the Guru Granth Sahib), copies of the 'My modern retelling' sheet on page 12 and coloured pens or pencils.

Plenary

Share the results from the activities.

- Ask a few of the children to share their work. Can the others say which story it is a modern retelling of? How do they know?
- Write some of the main points on the board. (You could use the format of the sheet on page 12.)
- What have the children learned about modern retellings?
- Was it difficult trying to keep to the same story but making it modern?

Extension activity

Look at stories of famous people from long ago (for example, Grace Darling, Florence Nightingale). Ask the children how these stories could be made into a modern retelling. Who would be the main character? Where would the story be set?

George and the wolf

George was a travelling salesman. He sold household items such as dusters, sprays and polish. He drove around the country knocking on people's doors with his suitcase full of surprises.

One morning he arrived in a village at the edge of a wood. It was a Saturday morning but the main street was deserted. George went into the local baker's shop to get a sandwich for his lunch. The shopkeeper shut the door behind him.

'It's very quiet today,' said George to the shopkeeper, 'What's going on?'

'Nobody dare go out on the street,' whispered the shopkeeper. 'There's a wolf roaming the village.'

'A wolf?' asked George. 'There's no such thing.'

'Ah, but there is,' replied the shopkeeper. 'It lives in the woods and it's the size of a donkey. It's chased the children in the playground and bitten farmer Wilson.'

Suddenly the door flew open and a woman rushed in with a pushchair.

'It's taken my baby!' she cried and pointed towards the wood. 'Help me!'

George put down his suitcase and set off towards the wood, afraid of nothing.

The wood was quiet and dark and still. George listened and looked. Then he saw it – a large dog the size of an Alsatian. By its side was a baby, still wrapped in its blanket, and a shopping bag. The dog was using its paws to search for food in the bag. It looked up when it saw George. He took the sandwich out of his pocket and showed it to the dog.

'Come on then,' he said gently to the dog. 'You're hungry aren't you, that's all.'

The dog slowly walked up to him and took the sandwich. Quickly George fastened a rope around its neck and tied it to a tree. Then he picked up the baby and ran back to the village.

The villagers clapped and cheered when they saw George with the baby.

'Don't worry,' said George. 'It's only a dog, a stray dog. It was hungry that's all.'

The villagers laughed. How could they have been afraid of a dog, a hungry dog!

Kinaesthetic learning

(Visual/Spatial, Linguistic, Intrapersonal, Naturalistic, Physical)

Make a comic strip

- Tell the children that they are going to draw their own comic strip for a children's comic. The strip will give a modern retelling of the story of David and Goliath from the Bible.

- Give them sheets of A3 paper divided into squares to look like a comic strip.

- Ask the children to read the story and think about how it can be put in a modern setting, for example by being set in a school with a bully and a bullied child.

- Hand out copies of the sheet on page 12 for them to write down their ideas.

- Tell the children to use coloured pens to draw pictures and then write speech bubbles to tell what happens. They should then give the story a title.

Auditory learning

(Interpersonal, Linguistic, Logical, Naturalistic)

Creating gossip about a saint

- Tell the children that they are going to imagine that they are telling a group of friends about something exciting that has happened based on the story of a saint (for example, St Francis or St Christopher).

- Give them a selection of stories about well known saints for them to read and choose one.

- Then ask them to write their ideas on the sheet on page 12 for a modern retelling of the story, remembering that it is gossip and so should be exaggerated. For example, 'You won't believe it but the other day I met a really wonderful man...'

- Encourage the children to tell their stories to each other using their notes.

- You could also arrange for the children to record their stories.

Visual learning

(Intrapersonal, Visual/Spatial, Linguistic, Physical, Naturalistic)

Write a news report

- Tell the children that they are going to write a news report using a story from a religious book such as the Bible, the Koran or the Guru Granth Sahib. For example, the story could be about someone getting healed.

- Provide them with the appropriate religious book and give them copies of the sheet on page 12 for them to write down their ideas.

- Encourage them to think of an exciting headline then to write the report using quotes.

- To finish, ask the children to draw a colour 'photo' for the report.

Name _____

My modern retelling

THINK ABOUT...
- Language
- Name changes
- Modern comparisons

IDEAS BANK

Saints   **Stories from famous old books**
St Christopher   Stories of Jesus
St Francis   Stories of Mohammed
                  Stories of the Sikh gurus
                  Stories of Buddha

Title of original story

_____

Title of new story

_____

Main characters

_____

_____

New characters

_____

_____

Setting

_____

Setting

_____

What happened

_____

_____

_____

_____

_____

What happens

_____

_____

_____

_____

_____

TEACHER'S NOTES

Playscripts

Whole class starter

- Give each child a copy of the text extract about Columbus on page 15 or display it on an OHP or interactive whiteboard.

- Tell the children that they are going to learn how to convert stories into playscripts. Together read the story and playscript.

- Ask the children the following questions.
    - Is the story modern or is it set in history? How do you know?
    - What is the story about?
    - Who was Columbus?
    - What is scurvy?
    - Why did sailors get scurvy?
    - What differences are there in the layout of the story and the layout of the playscript?
    - Look at the playscript. Some of the words are in brackets. What do they tell us? Why are they in brackets?
    - Which do you prefer – the story or playscript? Why?
    - What difficulties might you experience converting a story into a playscript?

Literacy objective

- To prepare a short section of story as a script.

What you need

- Photocopies of pages 15 and 17
- Coloured pens or pencils
- A selection of history books and books about different religions
- A2 paper cut in half lengthways
- Coloured A4 paper
- White A4 paper

> **Extension activity**
>
> Choose a famous event in history (for example, The Great Fire of London or The Battle of Hastings). Ask the children to discuss with a partner whether it is possible to convert the story into a play. What difficulties might there be? For example, if the story is set in a number of different places, or if it is difficult to produce the scene on a small stage.

Independent/group work

From the activities on page 16 either:

- select the most appropriate activity for each child/group according to whether they are kinaesthetic, auditory or visual learners and organise three separate working groups

or

- begin with the kinaesthetic activity for the whole class, then progress to the auditory and finally the visual activity over several lessons.

Tell the children that they are now going to work on their own playscripts.

The kinaesthetic learners will need:
A2 paper cut in half lengthways, copies of the 'My playscript' sheet on page 17 and some history books.

The auditory learners will need:
books about different religions and copies of the 'My playscript' sheet on page 17.

The visual learners will need:
coloured A4 paper, white A4 paper and copies of the 'My playscript' sheet on page 17.

Plenary

Show the results from the activities.

- Is it easier to convert an actual story rather than a piece of information from history into a playscript?
- What do you have to remember when converting a story into a play?
- What were some of the difficulties?
- What have the children learned about converting stories into playscripts?

Columbus and the scurvy

Excerpt from the book

The journey to America was proving difficult for Columbus, the Italian explorer, and his crew. Many of the sailors were ill and unable to work. Columbus was in his cabin feeling very sick.

'Would you like anything, Sir?' asked one of the cabin boys politely.

'Get me the ship's doctor now!' shouted Columbus from his bunk.

There was a knock at the door. It was the doctor. He opened the door and walked in.

'What's the matter?' he asked.

'I think I've got scurvy,' replied Columbus, showing the doctor the spots on his arms.

'We must get to land and stock up with fresh fruit and vegetables,' replied the doctor.

'And wh…what if we don't?' stuttered Columbus taking hold of the doctor's arm.

'We'll die!' replied the doctor clearly. 'We'll all die!'

Excerpt from the playscript

Narrator: The journey to America was proving difficult for Columbus, the Italian explorer, and his crew. Many of the men were ill and unable to work. Columbus was in his cabin feeling very sick.

Cabin boy: (*politely*) Would you like anything, Sir?

Columbus: (*shouting from his bunk*) Get me the ship's doctor now!
(*Knock, knock*)

Doctor: (*walking onstage*) What's the matter?

Columbus: I think I've got scurvy! (*showing the doctor the spots on his arms*)

Doctor: We must get to land and stock up with fresh fruit and vegetables.

Columbus: (*taking hold of the doctor's arm and stuttering*) And wh… what if we don't?

Doctor: (*clearly*) We'll die! We'll all die!

Kinaesthetic learning
(Physical, Linguistic, Visual/Spatial, Intrapersonal)

Make a concertina playscript
- Tell the children that they are going to work on their own to produce a concertina playbook.

- Give each one some coloured pens or pencils and a long piece of paper (A2 in length but half the height) and show them how to fold it to make a concertina book (at least six pages).

- Tell the children to choose a period of history with which they are familiar and to convert a story from that period into a play. Give them copies of the 'My playscript' sheet on page 17 to help them and make available a selection of history books.

- Ask the children to write the lines said by one of the characters (for example, Queen Victoria: 'I am not amused') on each page, and to draw a picture to accompany them.

Auditory learning
(Interpersonal, Linguistic, Physical)

Act it out
- Tell the children that they are going to work in small groups to produce a playscript from a religious story.

- Ask them to choose a story they know well and to list all the characters in the story.

- Then ask them to work together in a group to produce a script for the story. Give them copies of the 'My playscript' sheet on page 17 to help them.

- When they have finished, invite them to read the original story to the class first, and then read their playscript.

- Encourage the listening children to comment on how similar the story is to the playscript.

Visual learning
(Intrapersonal, Linguistic, Visual/Spatial)

Publish a book
- Tell the children that they are each going to write an historical playscript and put it inside a cover to look like a real book (for example, a book called Evacuation or The Blitz).

- Give them coloured A4 paper for the cover and white A4 paper for the text pages.

- Ask them to create an attractive cover.

- Inside the book they should write the story and then on a clean sheet of paper write the playscript. Give them copies of the 'My playscript' sheet on page 17 to help them.

Name _____

My playscript

Title of story/play
_____

Setting (scene)
_____

The story (notes)
_____
_____
_____
_____
_____
_____
_____
_____

Characters
_____
_____
_____

THINK ABOUT...
Facts about playscripts
- Character names are written on the left-hand side.
- Names start a new line when they speak.
- Don't use speech marks.
- There is no use of 'he said'.
- Brackets are used for stage directions and prompts for actors.

Prompts for the actors
(written in brackets)

shakily

stammering

happily

loudly

wearily

aggressively

politely

forcefully

stammering

whispering

Biographies

TEACHER'S NOTES

Literacy objective
- To develop the skills of biographical writing.

What you need
- Photocopies of pages 20 and 22
- Frieze paper or large sheets of paper
- Internet access
- A printer
- Scissors and glue
- A range of history books
- Encyclopedias
- Coloured pens or pencils

Whole class starter

- Give each child a copy of the biography of Henry VIII on page 20 or display it on an OHP or interactive whiteboard.

- Tell the children they are going to work on biographies. Ask them to tell you what a biography is. Write their ideas on the board. Now read the biography about Henry VIII.

- Ask the children the following questions.
  - What is the difference between a biography and an autobiography? (You could have available examples of both to show to the children.)
  - Why is the title so important?
  - This extract about Henry VIII is a biography. How do we know? Underline the words in the text that show it is a biography (he, his).
  - If this were an autobiography, what words would be different? ('He' would be 'I'.)
  - Why are there no quotes from people who were alive at the time? (Because it was written recently and the period was long ago so all the people who might have given quotes are dead.)
  - How do quotes improve a biography?
  - How has Henry VIII been seen through the ages?
  - Does the writer see Henry VIII as a good or bad character? Does the writing show any bias?
  - What does the writer say to make us believe he was a good man? Find the evidence.
  - After reading the information what is your opinion of Henry VIII?

TEACHER'S NOTES

Independent/group work

From the activities on page 21 either:

- select the most appropriate activity for each child/group according to whether they are kinaesthetic, auditory or visual learners and organise three separate working groups

or

- begin with the kinaesthetic activity for the whole class, then progress to the auditory and finally the visual activity over several lessons.

Tell the children that they are now going to work on biographies.

The kinaesthetic learners will need:
frieze paper (or the back of wallpaper) or large sheet of paper, Internet access, a printer, scissors and glue.

The auditory learners will need:
a range of history books and copies of the 'My biography' sheet on page 22.

The visual learners will need:
non-fiction books and encyclopedias.

Plenary

Share the results from the activities.

- How important is it to be clear in what you say or write when writing a biography?
- How can you persuade someone to believe what you write in a biography?

Extension activity

Arrange for the children to visit the local library to find out more about the characters they have been studying. Alternatively, ask them to write a biography about a child in their class. Encourage them to ask other children for quotes to include in their biography.

The real Henry VIII

Henry VIII was probably one of the most famous kings in history. But what was this man really like? Was he the man history books portray as mean and ruthless? Was he extravagant? Was he impatient and thoughtless? Or was he a man with a real heart, a man whose only dream was to have a son, a son to be king after he died? This is the real Henry VIII, a man for all seasons.

Henry was born in Greenwich in London. He was a clever boy and learned to speak several languages. He was very musical and played several instruments to the delight of family and friends. He was tall and strong and very good at sport including jousting, hunting and tennis. He liked to be with people and although he was competitive he was fair and always gave one hundred per cent.

Henry VIII became king when he was only eighteen. This was a trial in itself, but he took to it with determination and dedication. His first wife, Catherine of Aragon, had four sons by him but they all died. He was heartbroken and eventually divorced her for Anne Boleyn whom he hoped would give him a son. However, she had a daughter and it was said that she was a witch, so there was no alternative but to have her executed. (This was normal procedure in Tudor times.)

He married Jane Seymour and she had a son but she died soon afterwards. Henry was devastated because he loved Jane. Henry now had a son, but because so many of his children had died when they were very young he wanted to have more sons to make sure there was an heir to the throne. So he married Anne of Cleves who was from Germany but they divorced quite soon because she was thoughtless and said mean and nasty things.

Henry then married Catherine Howard. He was thirty years older than her. She had lots of young male friends who upset Henry and made him jealous. Women were expected to be loyal and only have eyes for their loved one. And after all, he was the king. He was so angry about it he had no alternative but to have her executed. In those days any king would have done the same.

His last wife was Catherine Parr. He was old and very ill when he married her. She loved him very much and took care of him until he died, devoted to the end.

Henry was not the ruthless king we read about. He didn't have his wives executed just because they didn't have sons. He cared deeply about people and some of them hurt him. If he was unkind why did Catherine stand by him to the end? She could have left. She could have deserted him, but no, she stayed with him because he had a heart. All he had ever wanted was a son to carry on his own name. He had feelings although life had let him down. This was the real Henry VIII.

Kinaesthetic learning
(Physical, Linguistic, Interpersonal, Visual/Spatial)

Make a wall display
- Tell the children that they are going to work together to produce a wall display about a famous character from history.

- Give them a roll of frieze paper or a very large sheet of paper.

- Ask the children to search the Internet to find sites about their character and then download some pictures.

- Ask them to assemble the images on the paper and underneath the pictures write about what they have found out.

Auditory learning
(Auditory, Linguistic, Intrapersonal)

Hot seating
- Tell the children that they are going to work on their own to investigate different characters from history, such as Tutankhamun, Christopher Columbus or Queen Victoria using non-fiction books.

- Give them copies of the 'My biography' sheet on page 22 to make notes about the characters.

- At the end of the lesson, invite each child to take the hot seat on the particular character they have chosen.

- Encourage the others to ask the child on the hot seat questions, using those on the 'My biography' sheet. Challenge the children to answer as many questions as possible correctly.

Visual learning
(Visual/Spatial, Linguistic, Intrapersonal)

Make a wanted poster
- Tell the children that they are going to work on their own to design a wanted poster for a famous character in history.

- Give them some coloured pens or pencils and sheets of A3 paper.

- Invite them to choose an historical character (maybe someone they have been studying in history such as Winston Churchill, Queen Victoria or John Lennon). Ask them to use a range of non-fiction books and encyclopedias to find out about their chosen character.

- When they have completed their research, tell them to create a wanted poster with a picture of the character and information about him or her around the edges. For example, 'Queen Victoria' – 'She was very serious', 'She wore black clothes'.

Name _____

My biography

Biography about
_____

The title of my biography
_____

Information about the character
_____
_____
_____
_____
_____
_____

Questions
- When did your character live?
- Where did he/she come from?
- What was he/she famous for?
- What were the high points of his/her life?
- Was he or she a good or bad person?

THINK ABOUT...
- Whether you are positive or negative about the character.
- Collect facts and evidence to support your view.
- Use rhetorical questions (those that don't need an answer, such as 'But was he happy?') to interest the reader.

How I feel about the character
_____
_____
_____
_____
_____
_____
_____

TEACHER'S NOTES

News reports

Whole class starter

- Give each child a copy of the newspaper report on page 25 or display it on an OHP or interactive whiteboard.

- Tell the children that they are going to work on news reports. Share some newspapers with them. Look at the kind of stories that are in newspapers. Consider the layout of the story – headline, picture, caption, introduction, information, quotation, credit line.

- Read the report together. Look at its features and discuss them. The story will answer the 4Ws (What? Where? When? Who?).

- Ask the children the following questions.
    - **What** is the report about?
    - **Where** is it taking place?
    - **Who** is it about?
    - **When** is it happening?
    - What are facts? What are opinions? Can you find them in the text?
    - What is the headline? Why is it important? Why are short headlines better than long ones?
    - Can you find the quotations?
    - How is the report laid out?
    - The report is written in paragraphs. How many paragraphs are there? When do you begin a new paragraph?
    - How is the introductory (lead) paragraph important? What should it contain? (A summary.)
    - Is there a byline?
    - Are there subheadings?

Literacy objective
- To write news reports.

What you need
- Photocopies of pages 25 and 27

Independent/group work

From the activities on page 26:

- select the most appropriate activity for each child/group according to whether they are kinaesthetic, auditory or visual learners and organise three separate working groups

or

- begin with the kinaesthetic activity for the whole class, then progress to the auditory and finally the visual activity over several lessons.

Tell the children they they are now going to work on their own news reports.

The kinaesthetic learners will need:
copies of the 'My news report' on page 27.

The auditory learners will need:
copies of the 'My news report' on page 27 and adults for interview such as the site supervisor and headteacher.

The visual learners will need:
copies of the 'My news report' on page 27.

Plenary

Share the results from the activities.

Ask the class to listen to the examples and think about the following:

- Did the reports include an introductory paragraph? What did they say?
- Is there evidence of quotations in the reports? Why are quotations useful?

Discuss the following:

- Why is the headline of a report so important?
- Why is the opening statement of a report so important?
- How did the practical activities help the children to write a formal news report?

Extension activity

Give each child a different headline that you have clipped from a local newspaper and a blank sheet of paper. Ask them to stick the headline at the top of the page and then write their own newspaper report using the headline.

Grillington Evening News

24 July 2002

WATER MADNESS!

Mark Jennings reports

A recent national survey has shown that more children each year are drowning outdoors.

Only this week, two children aged ten and eleven were drowned in Grillington Reservoir. They were alone in a rubber dinghy when it capsized.

This summer, a survey undertaken by the Water Safety Foundation has found that figures have doubled since last year. Rod Hudson a spokesman for The Water Safety Foundation said, 'There are far too many children who are unable to swim. It is the schools' duty to teach their pupils.'

The DfES blames schools

A spokesperson for the Department for Education and Skills said that they gave advice to schools on the standards of swimming expected when a child leaves primary school and that it is up to the schools to carry it out.

Teachers blame parents

Jan Barnes, chairperson for the Headteachers' Union said, 'It is not the schools' fault. Headteachers follow government guidelines and send children for swimming lessons. It is the fault of some irresponsible parents who allow their children to swim in freezing cold lakes and reservoirs. They should have more sense.'

Jan Barnes, chairperson for the Headteachers' Union said, 'It is not the schools' fault.'

A new advertising campaign

The government is trying to reduce the problem and a new advertising campaign about water safety will begin later this month.

Too late for Sam and Kevin!

It is too late for Sam Wilson and Kevin Pearson. If they'd seen the advertising campaign, maybe they'd be alive today!

Kinaesthetic learning
(Interpersonal, Physical, Linguistic, Logical)

Prepare a radio report
- Tell the children that they are going to work in a group to prepare a live radio report in response to the news report 'Water Madness'.

- Tell them that they need to ask the children in their group to respond to the news report by defending the families and children and putting blame on others.

- Help them to decide who is going to be the reporter and which children are going to play the interviewees – for example, Mrs Jones (mother) and Paul Smith (child).

- Ask the children to use the 'My news report' sheet on page 27 to jot down their ideas for the headline, story, picture and caption. Remind them to use the 4Ws to help them.

- Each child should prepare a quote for the report – for example, 'There should be more danger signs' and 'Children aren't having enough swimming lessons'.

- Invite the children to act out the report for the class as if it was being broadcast live on radio.

Auditory learning
(Interpersonal, Linguistic, Logical)

Make an interview
- Tell the children that they are reporters and they are going to interview the school site supervisor and headteacher about the dangers of playing on roofs. (Prime the adults about the interview.)

- Ask the children to jot down questions for the interview. Encourage them to share their ideas and choose the questions they wish to ask.

- Remind them that, as they interview the adults, they should make a note of the answers to the questions they have asked.

- When they have completed their interviews, ask them to write a report together about what they have found out, using the 'My news report' sheet on page 27.

Visual learning
(Visual/Spatial, Interpersonal, Intrapersonal, Linguistic, Logical)

Write a report
- Tell the children that they are going to work in pairs to write a newspaper report about the danger of playing on building sites. They should use a copy of the 'My news report' sheet on page 27 to help them.

- Encourage them to discuss the dangers in pairs and makes notes using the 4Ws to plan the report.

- Ask them to think up a quotation to appear in the report.

- Finally, ask the children to think of an exciting headline for their story.

Name _____

My news report

THINK ABOUT...
- The 4Ws – Who? Where? When? What?
- Headline
- Introductory paragraph
- Quotations
- Facts and opinions
- A byline
- A caption
- Subheadings

TEACHER'S NOTES

Science fiction genre

Literacy objective
- To study in depth one genre and produce an extended piece of similar writing.

What you need
- Photocopies of page 30
- Frieze roll (pale colour)
- Paint and brushes
- Photocopies of page 32
- A5 paper
- Stapler and staples
- Drawing materials

Whole class starter

- Give each child a copy of 'The globules!' sheet on page 30 or display it on an OHP or interactive whiteboard.

- Tell the children that they are going to be working on a particular writing genre. What genres do they know? List their examples on the board. Answers might include science fiction, adventure and humorous.

- Read the 'The globules!' sheet together. Now ask the children the following questions.
    - What kind of genre is this?
    - How do we know? List the features that show that this is science fiction (for example, the use of incredible gadgets, it is set in the future, there are encouters with aliens, the use of technical vocabulary and the use of a sinister mood).
    - Where is the story set?
    - What year is it?
    - What happens?
    - Why could the humans not defeat the aliens?

- Ask the children to find some evidence of scientific language in the text. Challenge them to think of some examples of their own.

- The writer uses adjectives and similes to create a visual picture. Ask the children to find examples of this. Tell them to shut their eyes and imagine what the aliens look like. How do they think the writer helps them to do this?

TEACHER'S NOTES

Independent/group work

From the activities on page 31 either:

- select the most appropriate activity for each child/group according to whether they are kinaesthetic, auditory or visual learners and organise three separate working groups

or

- begin with the kinaesthetic activity for the whole class, then progress to the auditory and finally the visual activity over several lessons.

Tell the children that they are now going to work on science fiction.

The kinaesthetic learners will need:
frieze paper, paint, brushes and copies of the sheet on page 32.

The visual learners will need:
A5 paper, stapler and staples and copies of the sheet on page 32.

Plenary

Share the results from the activities.

- What have the children learned about writing science fiction?
- Why is descriptive language so important in stories like this?
- How do the children know if they have been successful?
- What do the children enjoy about each other's stories?
- What makes a good science fiction story?
- Write their ideas on the board.

Extension activity

Watch a science fiction video that the children are unlikely to have seen. Show the first half of the film then ask the children to write the rest of the story. Compare stories. How are they different? How are they alike?

The globules!

It was the year 2099. It all began when a small bubble floated down from the sky, just like the bubbles children blow. It landed on a tree and burst, but it didn't disappear. The inside of the bubble was full of a clear liquid that trickled down the tree like a winding stream. It reached the ground and then wound its way across the land like a desert snake towards the town.

As it went, globules of fat jumped out from the liquid. The globules expanded and changed shape. They billowed up like melting candle wax to the size of small men. You could see their insides with veins like rivers of white blood, moving fast. They had transparent heads. They were smooth and elongated. They had no ears or noses but they had eyes like pink marbles that throbbed incessantly.

Two boys followed the globules. To them it was like being in the films they had seen or comic books they had read. At first they were excited but then became afraid. They hid behind a tree hoping the globules hadn't seen them. Their hearts were pounding and their eyes staring like cats. They tried to be still, but just one twig cracking under their weight alerted the globules.

Soon the boys were surrounded. They tried to shout. They tried to scream. But their cries were unheard. The globules swallowed them whole, then moved on.

Soon there was an army of them. They flowed into town, picking up speed as they went, getting stronger by the minute. Anything or anyone in their way was enveloped and gorged, disappearing inside their skins like a mincer. Soon the city was in panic with everyone trying to escape, but the aliens could see them with their ferret-like eyes and had them cornered in seconds.

The army was called out. They had speed tanks and armoured rollers but even when they squashed the globules, they sprang up again, unbeaten. They used the latest disintegrator sprays but they wouldn't dissolve the globules, even when the power source was set at maximum. They used their supersonic rifles but the microbullets went straight through the globules. They used lasers but with no effect. The globules were indestructible.

By nightfall the city was quiet. This was only the beginning.

Kinaesthetic learning
(Visual/Spatial, Linguistic, Interpersonal, Physical)

Making and using cut-outs
- Tell the children that they are going to work together to make life-size cut-outs of aliens.

- Give each pair of children a piece of frieze paper the length of a child. Ask them to work in pairs to draw an alien and then paint it.

- While the paintings are drying, give them copies of the sheet on page 32 and ask them to use it to describe the alien and what it does – for example, 'it melts people' or 'it can be exterminated with X-ray guns'.

- When the paintings are thoroughly dried, ask the children to work in their pairs to arrange the information about the alien around the image.

Auditory learning
(Interpersonal, Linguistic, Logical)

Make a live report
- Tell the children that they are going to work together to present a live report to the nation about the alien invasion. They are going to carry on from where the story ended.

- Tell each child that they are going to report on a different stage of the invasion. They will need to discuss what happens in each stage of the invasion and decide the order of speakers. They will need to make notes.

- Invite them to perform the news for the rest of the class – for example, 'The aliens entered the school. The school was unable to evacuate in time. Not one child or adult has survived.'

- Invite the 'reporters' to sit at your desk to look like real reporters in a studio.

Visual learning
(Intrapersonal, Visual/Spatial, Linguistic, Physical)

Write a diary
- Tell the children that they are going to work on their own to write a diary of an alien invasion.

- Give each child several sheets of A5 paper stapled together (to look like a real diary).

- Ask them to describe the invasion from beginning to end and to draw pictures for each diary entry using their own ideas or those on page 32.

Name _____

My science-fiction story

My ideas

_____

_____

_____

_____

_____

_____

Sketch

IDEAS BANK

Useful vocabulary
lasers
X-ray guns
zappers
bioblasters
exterminators
grunge guns
power sorters

Description of aliens
one-eyed
skin like metal
wrinkled
metamorphic
bulbous

The aliens' strengths

The aliens' weaknesses

THINK ABOUT...
- Setting
- Scientific vocabulary
- Descriptive language
- Pace and excitement
- Conclusion

TEACHER'S NOTES

Flashbacks

Whole class starter

- Give each child a copy of the 'Christmas lights' story on page 35 or display it on an OHP or interactive whiteboard.

- Tell the children that they are going to work on flashbacks. Ask if any of them know what 'flashback' means. Encourage them to share their ideas but do not come to any agreement yet. Write their ideas on the board.

- Now read the story with the children. Tell them that it contains a flashback. Agree that a flashback is a sudden recollection of something that happened in the past. In this story the flashback is of the fire at the house in the country and how the storyteller's father had his hands badly burned.

- Ask the children the following questions.
    - What is the story called?
    - Where is it set?
    - What is it about?
    - What made the flashback happen?
    - How did the author make it obvious to the reader that it was a flashback? (The words 'I was nine when it happened.')
    - What kind of experiences may bring on a flashback? Are they always bad ones or can they be good as well? Could it be linked to an object such as a toy or a person or a place? Write the ideas on the board.
    - Has anyone had a flashback? (You may need to deal sensitively with some children's responses.)

Literacy objective

- To use flashbacks to convey the passing of time.

What you need

- Photocopies of pages 35 and 37
- Objects linked to seasonal occasions – for example, Christmas decorations, wrapping paper, a chocolate egg, an old firework, a birthday card
- Magazines
- CDs of popular music and CD player
- Scissors and glue

TEACHER'S NOTES

Extension activity

Ask the children to write about a flashback they have experienced.

Give each pair of children an old photograph. Ask them to write a flashback imagining they have just seen the photograph. How different are the ideas even though each pair has the same photograph?

Independent/group work

From the activities on page 36 either:

- select the most appropriate activity for each child/group according to whether they are kinaesthetic, auditory or visual learners and organise three separate working groups

or

- begin with the kinaesthetic activity for the whole class, then progress to the auditory and finally the visual activity over several lessons.

Tell the children that they are now going to do some work using flashbacks.

The kinaesthetic learners will need:
seasonal objects (for example, Christmas decorations, wrapping paper, a chocolate egg, an old firework, a birthday card) and copies of the 'My flashback' sheet on page 37.

The auditory learners will need:
a variety of CDs with popular songs, a CD player and copies of the 'My flashback' sheet on page 37.

The visual learners will need:
magazines, glue and scissors.

Plenary

Share the results from the activities.

- Was it easier for the children to write about the flashback or talk about it? Why?
- What other objects may cause a flashback?
- How did the children make it obvious to the reader where the flashback occurs?
- Can the children think of any books they have read that have included a flashback? You could make a display of these books.
- Why don't we very often see the use of flashback in stories for younger children?

Christmas lights

It was my first year in the city. It wasn't at all like where we lived before. I wasn't used to the tall buildings, the traffic and the smog. I wasn't used to a house without a garden. It did however have some benefits. There were enormous shops with the latest toys and there were things to see and do, like bowling and going to the cinema.

It was our first Christmas in the city. I was really excited because it was the last day of school so I ran all the way home. When I walked into the kitchen I could smell mince pies in the oven. Mum was brilliant at baking. I threw down my bag and ran into the lounge.

'Mum, Mum,' I shouted excitedly. Then I saw it! The Christmas tree. The Christmas lights. I turned and fled.

I was only nine when it happened. We were a happy family then, living in the countryside. We'd been decorating the tree. Dad found some tree lights in a box and Molly, my little sister, was trying to help.

'They'll do,' said Dad smiling.

We helped him put them up. At first they wouldn't work so Dad fiddled around with the switch. He was good with his hands. He had made me a tree house and a go-cart when we lived in the country. Then the lights came on. Molly was really excited. She jumped up and down, shouted and squealed. All evening Molly stayed by the tree until it was time for bed.

'Look!' she kept shouting. 'Fairies!'

That night there was a fire. The lights were faulty and a single spark had caught the curtain. By the time we awoke, the whole of the downstairs was on fire. Mum took me by the hand and led me downstairs. Dad went to wake Molly. He managed to get into her room but then there was an explosion. Mum and I waited in the garden looking up at the flames. Dad appeared a few minutes later with Molly in his arms. But his lovely hands were black and badly burned. He still has the scars today. I will never forget those lights on the Christmas tree.

Kinaesthetic learning
(Intrapersonal, Kinaesthetic Linguistic, Logical)

Retelling a flashback
- Tell the children that they are going to work on their own to perform a flashback.

- Provide a variety of seasonal objects such as Christmas decorations, wrapping paper, a chocolate egg, an old firework, a birthday card.

- Invite each child to choose one object and think of how it could become the focus of a flashback – for example, the firework could remind them of a bonfire night when there was a dreadful accident or a birthday card could remind them of a lovely time they had with a special person.

- Give the children copies of page 37 to help them make notes about their ideas.

- Invite the children to perform their flashbacks to the rest of the class. For example, 'It was my birthday. I heard a knock at the door...'

Auditory learning
(Musical, Intrapersonal, Linguistic, Logical)

Using music
- Tell the children that they are going to talk through their flashback using a piece of music as a stimulus.

- Provide a variety of CDs with music the children will know. Let them play the CDs and choose one piece of music that will be their stimulus. (If headphones are available let the children work in groups with several pieces of music according to their preference.)

- Then on their own they should use a copy of page 37 to help them note their ideas that link the piece of music to an event in their past (for example, a funeral or a leaving party). They could begin their writing like this 'I was listening to the radio and suddenly my special song was played...'

- Invite each child to tell their story while their chosen piece of music is played in the background.

Visual learning
(Intrapersonal, Linguistic, Visual/Spatial)

Using a picture
- Tell the children that they are going to use a picture as a stimulus for a flashback.

- Provide plenty of magazines with pictures they can cut out – for example, places or animals. (Sunday supplements are useful.)

- Ask each child to choose a picture and stick it on a sheet of paper.

- Underneath the picture, ask them to write their flashback, imagining they have just seen the picture. For example, 'Someone had left an old photo album on the table. I opened it...'

- Invite the children to show their flashback pictures and read their writing to the rest of the class.

Name _____

My flashback

Where the story takes place
_____

What was happening at the time
_____
_____
_____

What caused the flashback
_____
_____
_____

What the flashback was
_____
_____
_____
_____

THINK ABOUT...
• **The setting**
home – school – a party
a friend's house
a garden – apark

THINK ABOUT...
What caused the flashback?
a birthday card
a Christmas decoration
a chocolate egg
an old firework

THINK ABOUT...
What happened?
an accident – a death
an injury – a fire
a flood – an explosion

TEACHER'S NOTES

Points of view

Literacy objective

- To draft and present a point of view.

What you need

- Photocopies of pages 40 and 42
- Large sheet of white paper
- Coloured pens
- Dictaphone
- Computer and printer

Whole class starter

- Give each child a copy of the letter on page 40 or display it on an OHP or interactive whiteboard.

- Tell them that they are going to work on points of view. They should be able to tell you what a point of view is and give examples.

- Tell them that the letter you are going to read is a balanced report. What do they think a balanced report is? Ask for their suggestions then read the letter together. Were they right?

- Ask the children the following questions.

    - Who is the letter to and from?

    - What is the letter about?

    - How is the topic introduced?

    - How do we know that it is a balanced report?

    - Write the heading 'for' on one side of the board and 'against' on the other. Agree points for each and list them underneath the headings.

    - How does the writer conclude the letter and why?

    - What words does the writer use to develop the argument – for example, 'however' and 'furthermore'. Ask the children to highlight or circle these words. Challenge them to think of other words that are similar.

TEACHER'S NOTES

Independent/group work

From the activities on page 41 either:

- select the most appropriate activity for each child/group according to whether they are kinaesthetic, auditory or visual learners and organise three separate working groups

or

- begin with the kinaesthetic activity for the whole class, then progress to the auditory and finally the visual activity over several lessons.

Tell the children that they are now going to work on points of view.

The kinaesthetic learners will need:
copies of the 'My point of view' sheet on page 42, a large sheet of white paper and coloured pens.

The auditory learners will need:
dictaphones and copies of the 'My point of view' sheet on page 42.

The visual learners will need:
copies of the 'My point of view' sheet on page 42, a computer and printer.

Plenary

Share the results from each activity.

- Ask the children if they think they achieved the objective. What did they do to achieve it?
- Ask them to share the words that helped to move the argument on. Write them on the board.
- What evidence did the children give to support their views.
- Is it easier to express a point of view on paper or verbally? Ask the children their opinions.

Extension activity

Encourage the children to write real letters expressing their point of view on a particular issue. They can write to:
- managers of local facilities
- managers of shops
- councillors
- the mayor.

Provide envelopes and stamps for the children to post their letters.

New leisure centre!

Franklin Road School
Peel Avenue
Lugton
LL3 4LY

12th September 2002

The Manager
Lugton Leisure Park
Lugton

Dear Sir

I am writing to congratulate you on the new leisure centre that opened last month. It has many positive aspects that the people of the town really appreciate. However, I thought that it was also important to inform you of some other aspects, which are not as positive.

Firstly, you should be commended on the actual opening of the centre. I, along with several of my friends, attended the opening. The free activities available all weekend were an excellent way of getting the local people interested. Furthermore, the free lessons given by the trainers were great fun.

Secondly, you should be commended on your competitive prices, which are far cheaper than other local centres, especially if you use the facilities in the evenings. However, people wishing to use them at weekends are having to pay twice the price, which is unsatisfactory.

My third point is concerning access to the leisure centre. It has a very large car park and is on a bus route; nevertheless, for people who cannot afford to use transport it is too far out of town to walk. Maybe you could offer a free minibus.

My final point is concerning the facilities. It has the best facilities I have ever seen. You can play any sport and there are lessons available. There are lots of family activities, too. However, as yet, you do not have any equipment for hire.

I hope you will find my letter useful and will consider some of my points for improving the centre even further.

Yours faithfully

Liam Connor

Kinaesthetic learning
(Interpersonal, Linguistic, Physical)

Produce a poster
- Tell the children that they are going to work together to produce a poster showing the positive and negative aspects of a facility in their own town – for example, an ice rink, a bowling alley or a cinema.

- When they have chosen the facility, give out copies of the 'My point of view' sheet (page 42) for them to jot down their ideas.

- Provide paper and coloured pens for them to create a poster with labels. The poster should feature a map of where the facility is, with labels showing positive/negative aspects of the location, and a drawing of the outside and inside of the facility with labels showing the positive/negative points.

- Encourage the children to colour the poster before presenting it to the rest of the class.

Auditory learning
(Interpersonal, Logical, Physical)

Make a telephone call
- Tell the children that they are going to have an imaginary telephone conversation with the manager of a local facility they all visit – for example, the local swimming pool.

- Arrange a visit to the chosen facility so that the children can investigate. Ask them to record their feelings about it using a dictaphone – for example, 'It's cheap but dirty'.

- When the children return to school, ask them to write down their ideas on copies of the 'My point of view' sheet (page 42).

- They can then set up an imaginary telephone conversation with the manager of the facility (who could be another child or an adult helper) telling him/her what they think of it (in a polite but constructive manner!).

Visual learning
(Intrapersonal, Linguistic, Visual/Spatial, Logical)

Write a letter
- Tell the children that they are going to work on their own to write a balanced letter to the manager of a facility in the town.

- Hand out copies of the 'My point of view' sheet (page 42) for them to note their ideas.

- Ask the children to type up their ideas on the computer and read their letters to the rest of the class.

Name _____

My point of view

THINK ABOUT...
- Both sides of the argument.
- Words to move the argument on.
- Facts and evidence.

Topic _____

Pluses/minuses	Evidence

Facilities

leisure centre
cinema
ice rink
bowling alley
swimming pool

Points

cheap/expensive
old/new/modern
high/poor
quality
clean/dirty
too busy/quiet

Useful words

firstly
secondly
thirdly
finally

Words to develop the argument

however
moreover
furthermore
nevertheless

TEACHER'S NOTES

Official language

Whole class starter

- Give each child a copy of the sheet on page 45 or display it on OHP or Interactive Whiteboard.

- Tell the children they are going to look at official language. Do they know what is meant by official language? Write down their ideas on the board but do not come to any conclusions.

- Read the letter together. Explain that it is written using official language. Ask the children the following questions.
    - Who is the letter to and from?
    - What is the letter about?
    - How is the letter different from one that you would send a friend?
    - Highlight the words and phrases that show us official language, for example 'advise', 'obliged' and 'proceed'.
    - Why are all the words important when you are writing an official letter?
    - Is descriptive language used? Why not?
    - On which other occasions would you use official language like this or hear official language like this? (In a court of law or a letter of complaint.)

Literacy objective

- To draft and present official language.

What you need

- Photocopies of pages 45 and 47
- A large piece of white paper
- Felt-tipped pens
- Old telephones
- A computer and printer

TEACHER'S NOTES

> **Extension activity**
>
> Imagine that you are a representative for the travel company and that you would like to contest what the holiday-maker has written about your company. You could do this as a letter to the holiday maker or as a statement to a television programme.

Independent/group work

From the activities on page 46 either:

- select the most appropriate activity for each child/group according to whether they are kinaesthetic, auditory or visual learners and organise three separate working groups

or

- begin with the kinaesthetic activity for the whole class, then progress to the auditory and finally the visual activity over several lessons.

Tell the children that they are now going to work on official language.

The kinaesthetic learners will need:
A copy of the sheet on page 47, dressing up clothes, such as a hat, glasses and coat.

The auditory learners will need:
A copy of the sheet on page 47 and old telephones.

The visual learners will need:
A copy of the sheet on page 47, a computer and a printer.

Plenary

Share the results from the activities.

Listen to the children's explanations. Discuss with them how accurate their explanations are. What words could have been deleted?

Ask the following questions.
- Why is accuracy important in official terms?
- What is the importance of official language?
- Under which circumstances do people use official language?

Name _____

A faulty phone

King Hill Electrics
Hill Street Business Park
Lyme Forum
LL2 4FY

30th December 2002					Our ref: B7F002564

Miss T Palmer
25 Park Drive
Lyme Forum

Dear Customer

We are in receipt of your mobile phone, which we received on 28th December. The machine has been thoroughly inspected by our technician.

A number of components have been diagnosed as faulty and, to restore operation, it will be necessary to repair it or, if in our opinion we deem it necessary, to replace it with a fully reconditioned model.

Unfortunately, we believe that the damage has been caused because it has been dropped in water. In light of this, we must respectfully remind you that the company does not accept liability. (See cover details for further information.)

As this work is not covered by warranty, we would advise the cost to be £95.95.

We would be obliged if you would consider the matter and favour us with your reply.

If you wish to proceed, please forward your cheque to the above address quoting our reference number.

We await your further instructions.

Yours faithfully

John Harold Howson

J H Howson
Customer Services Manager

Kinaesthetic learning
(Intrapersonal, Linguistic, Physical)

Act it out
- Tell the children they are going to work in pairs and imagine that one of them is a customer who has bought an item of clothing that is damaged, for example has a broken zip or the material is frayed, and the other is the shop manager.

- They plan and rehearse the conversation they would have, with each of them putting across their point of view using official language, such as 'It is store policy that…' and 'Furthermore…'

- They can use aids to help them get into character, such as a jacket and glasses.

- They can use the sheet on page 47 to help them make notes of the official language they are going to use.

- They should perform their conversation to the rest of the class.

Auditory learning
(Interpersonal, Linguistic, Logical, Physical)

Plan and hold a telephone conversation
- Tell the children they are going to work in pairs to plan an imaginary telephone conversation with the manager of the mobile phone company, complaining that they will have to pay to have their phone repaired when it is not their fault it is broken.

- Give them copies of the sheet on page 47 so that they can make notes about what they are going to write and pay particular attention to the words they are going to use.

- Each pair should demonstrate their agreed conversation to the rest of the class, making sure they use official language.

Visual learning
(Intrapersonal, Linguistic, Visual/Spatial, Logical)

Write a letter
- Tell the children they are going to work on their own to plan and write a letter of complaint to a travel company about a holiday that was not satisfactory.

- Give them copies of the sheet on page 47 so that they can make notes about what they are going to write and pay particular attention to the words they are going to use.

- When they have planned their letters they can use the computer to write them up and a printer to print them out. They should then read their letters to the rest of the class.

Name _____

Official language planner

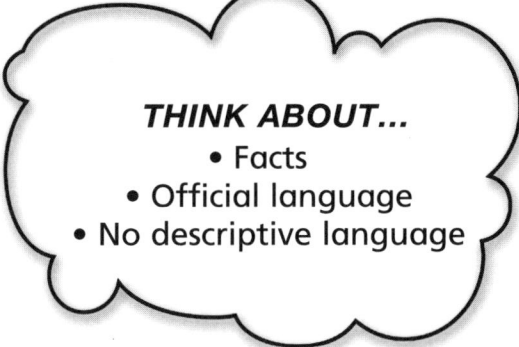

THINK ABOUT...
- Facts
- Official language
- No descriptive language

Introduction

Important points

-
-
-
-
-

Conclusion

Useful official language

receipt
inform
advise
remind
oblige
request
consider
accept
proceed

Holiday complaint

Late flight
Food – cold, flies
Room – broken furniture, plumbing
Hotel – pool, broken tiles, dirty

Faulty clothing

- ripped
- broken
- frayed
- shrunk in wash
- loose stitching
- colour faded in the wash

TEACHER'S NOTES

Writing blurb

Literacy objective

- To create blurb for a text or film.

What you need

- Photocopies of pages 50 and 52
- A collection of book covers
- Sticky notes
- A short children's film, television and video player
- A large sheet of paper
- A4 white paper
- Frieze paper
- Coloured pens

Whole class starter

- Give each child a copy of the back cover blurb on page 50 or display it on an OHP or interactive whiteboard.

- Tell the children they are going to create their own blurb. Do they know what blurb is? Write down their ideas on the board but do not come to any conclusions. Read the blurb together.

- Ask the children the following questions.
    - What is a back cover blurb?
    - Where would you find a back cover blurb?
    - What kind of book is this a back cover blurb for?
    - What is the story about?
    - Why would there be a brief outline of the story on the back cover?
    - Who gives their opinions of the book on the back cover? Why is this done?
    - Why is there an excerpt of the book on the back cover?
    - What information are you given? And from which sources?
    - What further information could have been given?
    - Who do you think would want to read this book?
    - Would you like to read this book? Why? Why not?
    - What age group would enjoy this book? Why?
    - What other things could blurb be written for? (Films, plays, playscripts and so on.)

TEACHER'S NOTES

Independent/group work

From the activities on page 51 either:

- select the most appropriate activity for each child/group according to whether they are kinaesthetic, auditory or visual learners and organise three separate working groups

or

- begin with the kinaesthetic activity for the whole class, then progress to the auditory and finally the visual activity over several lessons.

Tell the children that they are now going to work on their own blurb.

The kinaesthetic learners will need:
frieze paper, white paper and coloured pens.

The auditory learners will need:
a short children's film, television, video player and large sheet of paper.

The visual learners will need:
copies of the photocopiable sheet on page 52 and A4 paper.

Plenary

Share the results from the activities.

- Did the children include all the necessary information?
- Why is it useful for the publisher to have positive comments on the back cover?
- Is the front cover of a book important? Why?
- How does a back cover help the reader to decide whether the book is for them?
- Do the children find it more interesting writing a blurb for a book they know or one they don't know?
- Was there any difference in writing blurb for a film than for a book? If so, what?

Extension activity

Give the children a selection of colour magazines and ask them to cut out a picture from one of them that would be suitable for a book cover and stick it on the right-hand side of a sheet of A3 paper. Tell them to imagine that it is the front cover of a book. Ask them to add the title of the book and the author's name and to write the back cover blurb on the left-hand side.

The Quest

By John Blackwell

Illustrated by Penny Draper

Ben Garnett, a ten-year-old boy from Lancashire, goes to Scotland to stay with his grandparents during the summer while his parents are away on business. He meets a girl called Carrie who lives in one of the fishermen's cottages down by the harbour. One day while he is on the beach, he finds a bottle with a message inside. It is a cry for help. Ben sets off with his new friend Carrie to solve the mystery. He encounters strange folk and strange legends set in the heart of Scotland.

The author, John Blackwell

> *The clouds scudded overhead as night drew in. The wind bellowed and the waves grew higher and higher.*
> *'We should turn back Ben, the sea's too rough,' shouted Carrie, her voice barely heard above the sound of the crashing waves.*
> *'No, no! I can see land in sight,' replied Ben with a determined look in his eyes.*
> *'What's that in the water?' screamed Carrie, throwing down her oar.*
> *'It's, it's...'*

'Magic, legends, adventure – the key to successful children's story writing.'
The Daily News

'You won't want to put it down until it's finished.'
Writers Guild

An emotive, descriptive, adventure story by the author of 'Black Night', winner of the Statesman Writers Award.

Kinaesthetic learning
(Physical, Linguistic, Interpersonal, Visual/Spatial)

Create blurb for a film
- Tell the children that they are going to make a large advertisement for a film. Explain that it must include some blurb. They can work in pairs or groups.

- Talk about advertisements they might have seen, such as one for a 'Harry Potter' or 'Star Wars' film. Discuss what was on the advertisement. Ask them to choose a film to create an advertisment for.

- Give them a long piece of frieze paper, some white paper and some coloured pens. They need to think about different aspects of the advertisement – heading, storyline, an excerpt, quotes and pictures – and write each aspect on a piece of paper.

- Finally, they should arrange the pieces of paper on the frieze paper to make an advertisement. Display this for the other to see and discuss.

Auditory learning
(Auditory, Visual/Spatial, Interpersonal, Linguistic)

Be a film critic
- Tell the children that they are going to discuss the blurb for a film.

- Show a (preferably short) film and ask the children to make notes during the viewing.

- When the film has finished, encourage the children to brainstorm ideas through discussion.

- Invite each child to contribute ideas for the blurb on a large sheet of paper.

- Ask the children to use the ideas they have gathered as a group to produce a blurb for the film.

Visual learning
(Visual/Spatial, Linguistic, Intrapersonal)

Write some book blurb
- Tell the children that they are going to write the back cover blurb for a book they know well. Have available a selection of storybooks for them to choose from.

- Ask them to choose a one of the books and to make notes on a possible back cover blurb on a copy of the sheet on page 52. They must not look at the original blurb.

- Give each child a sheet of paper. Ask them to write the book's title, author's name, synopsis, an excerpt from the book, quotes from newspapers, and so on.

- Invite them to complete the blurb by drawing a picture that depicts the book.

- Compare the children's blurb with the book's actual blurb. How well does theirs compare?

Name _____

My back cover blurb

Title of book

_____

Author

_____

Illustrator

_____

> **THINK ABOUT...**
> - A clear summary
> - An exciting extract with suspense
> - Positive quotes

Synopsis

_____

_____

_____

Excerpt from the book

_____

_____

_____

_____

Quotes

_____

_____

_____

_____

TEACHER'S NOTES

Extended stories

Whole class starter

- Give each child a copy of the 'Tricks' story on page 55 or display it on an OHP or interactive whiteboard.

- Tell the children that they are going to work on extended stories. Read the story with them. Say that this has been specially written to show them that an extended story more often than not contains several chapters. This example only contains three miniature chapters on one page so that they can quickly get an idea in the starter session of what an extended story might look like. Show them some longer storybooks that have several chapters. Point out that normally each chapter will be a page or more long.

- Ask the children the following questions.
    - Why is the story called 'Tricks'?
    - What is the theme for the story?
    - What are the settings for the story?
    - What happens in each miniature chapter?
    - If you had extended the story further, what else could you have written?

Literacy objective
- To create an extended story, worked on over time on a theme identified in reading.

What you need
- Photocopies of pages 55 and 57
- Circus props (for example, a red nose, a toddler's tricycle, a silly hat or pair of trousers)
- Tape recorder/dictaphone
- Computer and printer
- Stapler and staples
- Coloured pens

Extension activity

Set the children a homework assignment over an entire half term to work on an extended story with the aim of filling an exercise book. Ask them to design a front cover for their story. Arrange for the children to present their books to the rest of the class at the end of the half term, and set up a 'lending library' for the children to borrow and read each other's stories.

Independent/group work

From the activities on page 56 either:

- select the most appropriate activity for each child/group according to whether they are kinaesthetic, auditory or visual learners and organise three separate working groups

or

- begin with the kinaesthetic activity for the whole class, then progress to the auditory and finally the visual activity over several lessons.

Tell the children that they are going to write their own extended stories with the themes of magic, the circus and animals.

The kinaesthetic learners will need:
copies of the story planning sheet on page 57 and circus props if available (for example, red nose, toddler's tricycle, silly hat or pair of trousers).

The auditory learners will need:
copies of the story planning sheet on page 57 and a tape recorder/dictaphone.

The visual learners will need:
copies of the story planning sheet on page 57, a computer, a printer, a stapler and staples and coloured pens.

Plenary

Share the results from the activities.

- What were the difficulties?
- Why was the planning so important?
- Who would the children's extended stories appeal to?
- What advice would the children give to someone writing an extended story?

Tricks

Chapter 1

The puppy lay on the river bank, its heart beating slowly. By its side was a plastic bag. The bag was open and there was something inside, but whatever it was didn't move. Every few seconds the puppy shivered and winced. Unable to move, it lay on the bank. It was not until late afternoon that two boys came by.

'Hey look, a puppy!' shouted the oldest boy.

The puppy opened his eyes and saw a round face with a head full of unkempt hair looking down at him. It was a boy of about eleven. The puppy tried to get up but its legs were so weak he fell down again. Another boy appeared. He was about five years old.

'I think someone tried to drown it,' said the boy with the round face, sadly.

The smaller boy nodded. Jack, the older boy looked in the bag and shivered. Two other puppies who had not been so lucky lay lifeless in the bag. Jack took off his jumper and wrapped it around the puppy.

'You're okay now,' he said gently. 'I'll look after you.'

Jack picked up the puppy and took him home.

Chapter 2

Within days the puppy had regained his strength. Jack found him a basket and put a blanket inside it and put it by the fire. He fed the puppy with warm milk and puppy food.

'What shall I call you?' asked Jack.

The puppy sat up and gave him his paw.

'You're a clever puppy,' said Jack. 'I know what, I'll call you Tricks!'

Tricks *was* a clever puppy. He could hold out his paw, sit, beg, roll over and even dance. Jack brought his friends over to see Tricks.

'Watch this!' said Jack excitedly to his younger brother, Harry, and all his friends.

Tricks sat up. One by one he did all the tricks Jack taught him. Every day the children from Jack's class came over to watch Tricks. He really was a clever puppy.

Chapter 3

One Saturday Harry woke up feeling ill. The doctor came and said he had the flu. Harry lay in bed for a week. He barely moved and slept most of the time. The doctor returned, looking concerned. Harry hardly had the strength to sit up and couldn't eat anything.

'I don't understand,' said the doctor. 'He should be feeling better by now.'

The doctor and Jack's mum sat in the kitchen wondering what to do. Jack suddenly had a great idea and ran upstairs. Suddenly Jack's mum heard laughing. She ran upstairs and saw a strange but wonderful sight. Tricks was on the bedside rug. He had a fancy collar around his neck and he was dancing to some music. Harry was clapping his hands. The wide smile on his face told everyone he was getting better. All it took was a dog and a few tricks!

Kinaesthetic learning
(Physical, Visual/Spatial, Interpersonal, Linguistic, Logical)

Write a story then mime it
- Tell the children that they are going to work in groups to create and act out an extended story with a circus theme for younger children.
- Hand out copies of the story planning sheet on page 57. They should agree some chapter headings – for example, The Clowns, The Acrobats, The Performing Animals, The Jugglers – and each child be allocated one chapter. They write down their chapter heading and then make notes about what might happen in each chapter.
- When they have written their ideas, they can read the group story to the rest of the class while the others mime the actions – for example, 'The Circus, Chapter 1. One day the circus came to town…'
- The children miming the story could use props – for example, a red nose, a toddler's tricycle, a silly hat/pair of trousers.

Auditory learning
(Linguistic, Physical, Intrapersonal, Logical)

Write a story for the radio
- Tell the children that they are going to work on their own to write an extended story for the radio called 'The Sorcerer' for children of their own age.
- Ask the children to write down their ideas for each chapter on a copy of the story planning sheet (page 57) and then record their story onto tape. (This may take time and they may only be able to record one chapter per lesson.)
- When they have finished recording their story, invite them to play it back to the rest of the class.

Visual learning
(Intrapersonal, Visual/Spatial, Linguistic, Logical)

Make a real book
- Tell the children that they are going to work on their own to produce an extended story called 'Drama at the Funfair' for a child their own age. The story should have at least three chapters.
- Hand out copies of the story planning sheet on page 57 and ask the children to write down their ideas.
- When they have completed their planning, each child should write the story on the computer and then create a picture for the front cover using clip art, if they are able.
- Show them how to assemble their book using a card front cover and stapled pages.

Name _____

My extended story

Title
_____

Chapter 1
_____
_____
_____
_____

Chapter 2
_____
_____
_____
_____

Chapter 3
_____
_____
_____
_____
_____

IDEAS BANK

Circus
clowns
acrobats
animals
jugglers

Funfair
games
prizes
stalls
rides
fortune teller
danger
stranger
emergency

Sorcerer
cauldron
spell
ingredients
creepy crawlies
invisible
shrink
magic wand

THINK ABOUT…
- The main characters
- The setting
- Themes for each chapter
- An interesting ending

TEACHER'S NOTES

Explanations

Literacy objective
- To secure control of impersonal writing through an explanation.

What you need
- Photocopies of pages 60 and 62
- Non-fiction books on electricity and magnetism
- Objects for kinaesthetic experiment on conductors – for example, metal, wood, card, plastic, battery, bulb, wires, crocodile clips
- Card
- Objects for auditory experiment on static electricity – for example, balloon, plastic comb
- Objects for visual experiment on magnets – for example, magnets, paper clips, needles, compass
- Large sheets of paper
- Coloured pens

Whole class starter

- Give each child a copy of the 'Electric circuits' sheet on page 60 or display it on an OHP or interactive whiteboard.

- Tell the children that they are going to be looking at explanations. Read the text together.

- Ask the children the following questions.
    - What do you notice about the way the explanation is set out? (It has an introduction, paragraphs and a diagram to explain the concept.)
    - What do you notice about the language? (It has factual information, it is clear and concise, it is impersonal, it is written in the present tense, it uses hypothetical language, it uses words/phrases to make sequential, causal, logical connections.)
    - Why do you think there is a diagram? How did it help your understanding of the idea?

TEACHER'S NOTES

Independent/group work

From the activities on page 61 either:

- select the most appropriate activity for each child/group according to whether they are kinaesthetic, auditory or visual learners and organise three separate working groups

or

- begin with the kinaesthetic activity for the whole class, then progress to the auditory and finally the visual activity over several lessons.

Tell the children that they are now going to work on their own explanations.

The kinaesthetic learners will need:
non-fiction books on electricity, a variety of objects for an experiment on conductors (for example, battery, bulb, wires, crocodile clips, metal, wood, card, plastic) and card for labels.

The auditory learners will need:
a variety of objects for an experiment on static electricity (for example, balloon, plastic comb, objects which hold static electricity) non-fiction books on electricity, copies of the 'My explanation' sheet on page 62.

The visual learners will need:
a variety of objects for an experiment on magnetism (for example, magnets, paper clips, needles, iron filings, compass and non-magnetic items such as pencils, plastic toys, wool and so on), non-fiction books on magnetism, copies of the 'My explanation' sheet on page 62 and large sheets of paper.

Plenary

Share the results from the activities.

- What have the children learned about explanations?
- Why is it important to be clear and concise?
- Why are diagrams important?

Extension activity

- Ask the children to write a simple explanation book for a younger child. Help them to think about the topic they will write about, the type of language they will use and what diagrams they will draw. Make available a variety of non-fiction books from the library to help the children. When they have made a simple book, arrange for them to read it to a group of younger children. Do the younger children understand the explanation? Is it at the appropriate level for their age?

- If the children have access to an interactive whiteboard, they could prepare a Powerpoint demonstration explaining a theory about electricity or magnets.

Name _____

Electric circuits

How does an electric circuit work?

Electricity must have a complete pathway to travel around. The pathway is called a circuit.

To make a circuit for a light, it is necessary to have a battery, a light bulb in a holder and two wires.

First you have to attach one end of each wire to the battery then you have to fasten the other end of each wire to the bulb holder.

When the wires are all connected, the electric current will flow from the battery and down the wire.

Then the current passes through the bulb and it lights up. The electricity carries on flowing back to the battery along the other wire and the light remains lit.

If part of the circuit is not joined up, the electricity will not flow at all. This can be tested by unfastening one of the wires.

The idea can be developed further by adding a switch.

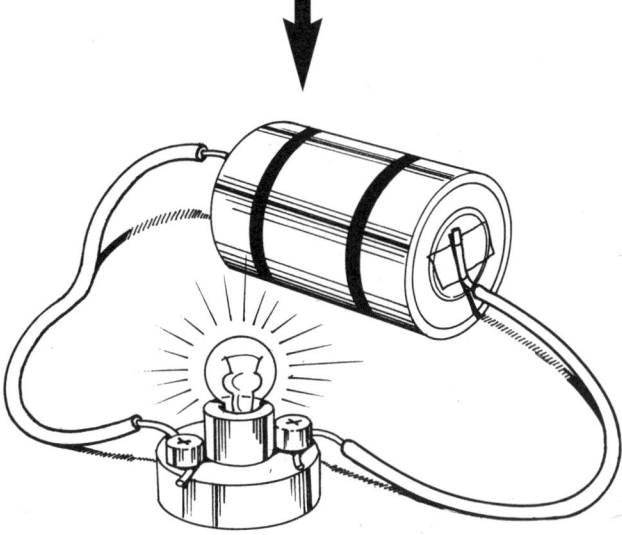

This principle applies to the electricity we have in our homes. Mains electricity needs a switch to turn it on or off. When the light is switched on, the circuit is completed and the electricity flows around. When the light is switched off the circuit is broken and the electricity stops flowing around.

Kinaesthetic learning
(Physical, Interpersonal, Linguistic, Visual/Spatial)

Make a labelled display on conductors
- Tell the children that they are going to work together in small groups or pairs to prepare a display with labels explaining how electric conductors work. (They should already have done some work on electricity.)

- Provide a range of non-fiction books about electricity and a variety of objects as conductors – for example, metal, wood, card and plastic. The group should discuss which objects conduct electricity and which do not.

- Ask them to set up their experiment as a display and write information labels on folded card to explain what happens, for example 'Metal objects conduct electricity.'

- Encourage the rest of the class to visit the display.

Auditory learning
(Linguistic, Physical, Interpersonal, Logical)

Demonstrate static electricity
- Tell the children that they are going to work together to imagine they are scientists giving a demonstration to their students on static electricity. The children can use a balloon that has been rubbed on a sleeve, plastic comb or other objects that hold static electricity.

- Provide a range of non-fiction books on electricity to help them.

- Ask the children to write their ideas for the presentation on copies of the 'My explanation' sheet on page 62.

- Invite them to present their explanation of static electricity to the rest of the class using the objects, for example 'Certain objects have static electricity. Take a balloon and run it up and down on your sleeve. This is what happens...'

Visual learning
(Inter/intrapersonal, Linguistic, Visual/Spatial, Logical)

Make an arrow chart about magnets
- Tell the children that they are going to produce arrow charts explaining magnets – for example, how magnets work, force fields or magnetic fields.

- Provide magnets, paper clips, needles and a compass as well as non-magnetic items.

- Have available non-fiction books or information sheets to help the children conduct an appropriate experiment.

- Ask them to jot down findings and ideas on copies of the 'My explanation' sheet on page 62 and then transfer these in more detail onto their own large sheet where they will draw large coloured arrows explaining the information in a step-by-step approach.

Name _____

My explanation

Question
_____

Explanation
_____
_____
_____
_____
_____
_____

Labelled diagram

WORD BANK

Conductors
battery
bulb
crocodile clips
light bulb
wire
paper clip
wood
card
plastic

Static electricity
balloon
sleeve
plastic comb
plastic
wood
metal

Magnets
paper clips
needle
compass
non-magnetic objects

THINK ABOUT...
• **choice of vocabulary**
if, then, might, when, while, during, after, because, due to, only, when, so

TEACHER'S NOTES

Non-chronological reports

Whole class starter

- Give each child a copy of the 'Tropical rainforests' sheet on page 65 or display it on an OHP or interactive whiteboard.

- Tell the children that they are going to be looking at non-chronological reports. Read the sheet together. Agree that a report tells us about something. Explain that a non-chronological report is one that can be written in any order. You don't lose the sense if you read the last paragraph first, unlike if you were reading a set of instructions.

- Ask the children the following questions.
    - What information does this report give us?
    - What are the features of a non-chronological report? (It has an introduction, headings and lots of factual information.)
    - What do you notice about the language? (It is impersonal and is written in the present tense.)
    - Read the introduction. What is an introduction? How is it different from the other paragraphs?
    - How many subheadings are there? What are they? Why are there headings?
    - How do headings help the reader?

Literacy objective
- To secure control of impersonal writing.

What you need
- Photocopies of pages 65 and 67
- Non-fiction books on endangered species, pollution and global issues
- A4 paper
- Crayons and coloured pens
- Frieze board or large paper
- Internet access and a printer
- OHT sheets

Extension activity

Challenge the children to investigate problems of the modern world. Ask them to do some research on the internet and collect their information in a scrapbook.

Independent/group work

From the activities on page 66 either:

- select the most appropriate activity for each child/group according to whether they are kinaesthetic, auditory or visual learners and organise three separate working groups

or

- begin with the kinaesthetic activity for the whole class, then progress to the auditory and finally the visual activity over several lessons.

Tell the children that they are now going to work on their own non-chronological reports.

The kinaesthetic learners will need:
non-fiction books about endangered species, A4 paper, crayons, coloured pens and covered frieze board (or large sheet of paper to display work).

The auditory learners will need:
non-fiction books about pollution and copies of the sheet on page 67.

The visual learners will need:
non-fiction books and magazines about global issues (such as global warming or acid rain), internet access, printer, copies of the sheet on page 67 and OHT sheets.

Plenary

Share the results from the activities.

- Ask the children what happens if the paragraphs are swapped around. (It does not matter because it is a non-chronological report.)
- With which type of writing would it make a difference if the paragraphs were moved around? (Instructions and explanations.)
- What have the children learned about non-chronological reports?
- Why is it important to include headings?
- Why are introductions important when writing reports?

Name _____

Tropical rainforests

Tropical rainforests are found across the world on either side of the equator. They stretch from Central and South America through Western Africa across Asia to northern Australia.

Climate
Tropical rainforests are warm, wet places with at least 200cm of rain each year.

Layers of the forest
There are different layers in the rainforest. The canopy is the highest part and is bathed in sunlight. The emergent layer is the next layer and further down is the under storey, which is warm and humid. The forest floor is surprisingly clear of vegetation. There are lots of animals that live on the forest floor.

Animals and plants
Millions of species of plants and animals live in the rainforest. Mountain gorillas, tigers and orang-utans live in the rainforest. The rainforests provide us with many important foods and medicine from many rare plants.

People of the forest
Rainforest people are dying out. They live a very simple life but as more trees are chopped down they have to move on.

Disappearing forest
The rainforests are disappearing because they are being cut down for wood and paper and some are burned by cattle ranchers. Over half of the tropical rainforests have gone. An area the size of 40 football pitches is destroyed every minute. As the rainforests disappear, the Earth's climate is affected, causing global warming. When rainforests are burned it causes acid rain, which is similar to the kind of pollution produced by factories. As the rainforests disappear, so too do the plants, animals and medicines that can save people's lives.

The disappearing rainforest is a shared problem for everyone and one that must be resolved soon before it causes the end of the human race!

Kinaesthetic learning
(Physical, Interpersonal, Linguistic, Visual/Spatial)

Make a wall display
- Tell the children that they are going to work together to produce a wall display about endangered species.

- Provide some non-fiction books about endangered species, A4 paper, crayons, coloured pens and a covered frieze board (or large sheet of paper).

- Ask each child to choose an endangered species, draw a picture of it and write about it underneath.

- Help the children to assemble their information on the wall to produce a non-chronological report display.

Auditory learning
(Linguistic, Physical, Interpersonal, Logical

Hold a debate
- Tell the children that they are going to work together to debate pollution.

- Provide them with a variety of non-fiction books about pollution.

- Allocate a different aspect of pollution (for example, river, sea, factory or traffic) to each child to investigate. Encourage them to consider the effect their type of pollution is having and how it can be resolved.

- Ask the children to note their ideas on a copy of the report sheet on page 67 and then produce a paragraph to read to the rest of the class, ready for a debate.

Visual learning
(Intrapersonal, Linguistic, Visual/Spatial, Logical)

Produce an OHT
- Tell the children that they are going to work on their own to produce an OHT for a class presentation on a global issue, such as acid rain or global warming.

- Provide some appropriate non-fiction books and magazines. Give the children access to the internet and ask them to make notes on the report sheet on page 67.

- They can also download pictures from the internet and photocopy them onto the OHT.

- Ask the children to use the pictures on the OHT to help them deliver their presentation as they read their information from their report sheet.

Name _____

My non-chronological report

Title _____

Introduction

_____

_____

_____

1st heading

_____

_____

_____

2nd heading

_____

_____

_____

_____

3rd heading

_____

_____

_____

_____

THINK ABOUT...
- a clear and simple introduction
- headings for each aspect of the topic
- factual information

IDEAS BANK

Endangered species
rhino
elephant
panda
peregrine falcon
mountain gorilla
parrot
blue whale

Pollution
sea
river
factories
nuclear
traffic

Food
allergic reactions
asthma
hyperactivity